Life Work

Also by Charlotte Mandel

Rock Vein Sky
Sight Lines
The Marriages of Jacob
Keeping Him Alive
The Life of Mary
Doll
A Disc of Clear Water
Saturday's Women
(editor, with Maxine Silverman and Rachel Hadas)

Life Work

poems by

Charlotte Mandel

*To Joan,
with affection,
Charlotte*

David Robert Books

© 2013 by Charlotte Mandel

Published by David Robert Books
P.O. Box 541106
Cincinnati, OH 45254-1106

ISBN: 9781625490308
LCCN: 2013941218

Poetry Editor: Kevin Walzer
Business Editor: Lori Jareo

Visit us on the web at www.davidrobertbooks.com

Cover photographs by Vincent Covello

Printed in the United States of America on acid-free paper

Remembering Manny

and for our children

and grandchildren

Acknowledgement with thanks to editors of the publications in which the following poems have appeared, sometimes in slightly different form.

Mezzo Cammin: "Life Work"; "Afternoon Rite; The Pond"
Prairie Schooner: "Split Screen"; 81.2 (Summer 2007), reprinted
    by permission of the University of Nebraska Press.
    Copyright 2007 by the University of Nebraska Press.
Tupelo Press Poetry Project: "Sight Loss" (the first line is by Petrarch),
    published by Tupelo Press, copyright 2009 Charlotte Mandel,
    used with permission.
Journal of New Jersey Poets: "Secret Model"; "Moving to a Smaller
    Home, I Give Up My H.D./Bryher Collection"; "Sweater";
    "Giving Up Teaching"
Verse Wisconsin: "News of the Day Pantoum"; "Inside/Outside:
    Gurgaon, India"; "Dream Spies"; "Abel, the First Funeral"
I-70 Review: "Tell Me the Names You Don't Know"; "New
    Child"; "Hall of Mammalian Life"; "Tell Me, Brother
    Dying"
Adanna: "Sea Chantey"
Umbrella: "The Amsler Grid Test"; "Spilled White"
Your Daily Poem: "Martha's Vineyard"; "Revelation"
Versal: "Tell Me, Pretty Maiden, Are There Any More At Home Like
    You?"
Bigger Than They Appear, Anthology: "Seven-Day Candle"
Rondeau Roundup: "Oak Tree Chronicle"; "Beachcomber"
Qaartsiluni: "The Mollusc World"
Poemeleon: "Rauschenberg's Goat"; "Hatshepsut, Woman-Pharoah"
Melusine: "Three El Greco Portraits"
The Crafty Poet: A Portable Workshop: "Flood Washed"

I am grateful to Colette Inez and Deena Linett for generous critical readings of the manuscript, and to Carol Nolde, and George Petty for insightful comments on poems in progress. Special thanks to my grandson Avi Shultz for invaluable technical assistance.

Table of Contents

I
Time Field 13
Life Work 14
Giving Up Teaching 21
On Fidelity 23
Afternoon Rite 24
Sleeping in Half a Bed 25
Crossing the Calendar Bridge 27
Dream Spies 30
Where I Live Now 31
Dried Reeds 32

II
Secret Model 37
Three El Greco Portraits 39
Ukiyo-e, Beauty in Woodblock Print 40
Rauschenberg's Goat 41
The Mollusc World 42
Hall of Mammalian Life 43
Hatshepsut, Woman Pharoah 45
Writers' Museum 47
Sculptor 48

III
Sight Loss 51
The Amsler Grid Test 53
Seven-Day Candle 54
Sweater 55
Tell Me the Names You Don't Know 58
Tell Me, Brother Dying 60
Moving to a Smaller Home, I Give Up My
       H.D./Bryher Collection 62
Stillness at 3:00 A.M. 64
Flood Washed 65

IV
News of the Day Pantoum 69
Split Screen 71
Awakening, She 72
Tell Me, Pretty Maiden, Are There Any More at Home Like
 You? 73
Sea Chantey 74
Milton's Daughters 75
Inside/Outside: Gurgaon, India 76
Beggars, We Pray in Flood 78
Abel, the First Funeral 79

V
New Child 83
Revelation 84
Martha's Vineyard 86
Beachcomber 88
The Pond 89
Oak Tree Chronicle 90
November, Woman and Birds 91
At the Vernal Equinox 92
Autumn Walk in a Gated Garden 93
Spilled White 95

About the Author 97

I

Time Field

The telephone ring that wakes me
stops—

a dream?   or were you
lifting the receiver

to a hotel wakeup call
three thousand miles away?

Listen, in bed before you left
as we turned toward each other
like gates closing for the night,

my hand on your chest, half-asleep

I stood at a bus stop reading signs
printed in an unknown alphabet

and you startled cried out
"Where are you going?"

I sat up.
Lampost light seeped in as always
through the window blinds.
You slept.

Which of us is mapmaker,
time-setter to our coupled lives?

A chart of blue lines superimposes
spaces traveled out of body.

Life Work
Interior: painting by Edouard Vuillard

    i

Muted, she disappears into background,
her dress a match in color and silence
to the wallpaper. Public words earn pained
downturns of parental mouths. Her defense
rests on camouflage, inner ear listening
for a train approaching town, slackening
speed, its unmistakeable warning whistle
by which she calculates, keeping track
counting numbers of engines crossing east
or west, tapping a foot to syncopate
her college beat—set out for either coast—
jack-out-of-box, life hers to orchestrate.
Red duffle packed, she'll mount the wheels alone.
No sense waiting for some prince to telephone.

ii

No prince, he calls from his college pay phone
at Sunday low rate. It isn't that they've
class news or gossip: subtleties of tone
report sweet, sour, ironic, fun. They crave
the heat of touch, use syllables to span
cold air. The wire opens trails where feelings flow
like steam from summer meadow after rain.
Contralto/tenor banter—quid-pro-quo
pattern for the future—pre-marriage play
disputing favorites—Jean Gabin
for her, Hedy for him. A chance to say
anything, nothing eases fear of joining.
Another's frown or smile cannot distract
the sensory self day-dreaming love acts.

iii

The sensory self day-dreaming love acts
with movie stars or neighbors will not break
promises of licensed social contract.
Unwritten rules work like fences. To slake
thirsts, close the bedroom door while children sleep.
Marriage their roof-tree, no leaks in rafters.
He drives to work, gives up smoking; she keeps
the kids clean, vaccinated. A letter
invites him to a Far East war. He tosses
it out. And a second. A third cries: "Greetings!"
Lottery lands him in the live oak mosses
of Virginia, practice swamp. Defeating
an enemy can't relax today's wars.
Jet smoke arrows the blue, asking: What for?

iv

Jet smoke arrows the blue sky, twin for-
mation, dissipates over barbed wire:
Truce. Home safe, they buy a house, G.I. mort-
gage. Though marriage rafters splinter, desire
re-glues. "Hey," they joke, "we're made of velcro—"
chest to chest, constructed to stick, pull, stick.
But the world spirals around—vertigo
has her holding on to doorways, afflicted
with agoraphobia as though a sea
has washed up the street, as though she must swim
to grocery, post office, library.
The word "love" dissolves to its antonym.
Meanwhile the children of a sudden grow
into strangely familiar people they know.

v

These strangely familiar people know
how to sweep back salt waters that linger
like a self-made lake of tears. Punctilio
filial pitch? No, their agile fingers
work the keyboards, ideas are summoned.
Marriage of Mom&Dad ends rivalry—
their talents linked towards a goal in common—
audit a sixtieth anniversary.
Earth rotates and the married numbers stun:
three hundred sixty five times sixty
equals twenty-one thousand nine hundred;
add fifteen leap years to the mix.
A banquet celebrates the count of days.
"He looks at you with love," the waiter says.

vi

"He looks at you with love," the waiter says.
Is that his line to couples as he pours
champagne to honor years slept in one bed?
What does his practiced eye perceive in demure
shared glances across a table of friends?
What's love? How may needy ardor marry
friendship? Their day-by-day achieves a blend
on low speed, converting tears and "sorry"
to dialogue of shrugs. Anger outgrows
its role as flint to erotic spark. Tonight,
on the verge of drift into undertow
of solitary dream, hands re-unite—
his gold ring's been lost, and hers is worn thin—
still—pulse beats echo wedding violins.

vii

The pillow transmits pulse beats—violin
vibrating pizzicato inside ear drums.
Unbutton pajamas—warm bony skin
to kiss. Limbs fall into sideward columns
of peace. Mind transposes the day's collage
into slides of honeymoon black and white
snapshots. Shuffle through glossy images
fading to sepia, history of bright
camera ready smiles...*barefoot on a rough
makeshift pier at the lake's edge, classic pose
swan dive, slim in profile... in air...* he coughs,
waking her, not himself. Rustle of bedclothes,
slow turnings. Breath has a feathery sound,
muted, disappearing into background.

Giving Up Teaching

In an academic library, the dry leaf
crackle of a turning page,
shuffle of a book taken down
put back,
snap of a laptop,
rubber soled footsteps.

I face the clock,
en route to teach a final
women's poetry workshop,
"an island of sanity".

Transition is a bridge to loss.
I'll miss the births, deaths,
motherings, angers, raptures,
sounded in their syllables,
the unpretentious wisdom
aglow in their faces.
We share a geography of decades
bordered by a "good" war
and the swamp or snow or sand-filled
ditches and hills of wars since.

Without that workshop's tonic island
shall I be a castaway
on the coast of old womanhood? Isolate,
allotted a fenced-in garden—the rose trellis
a straggle of thorned vines, the beds of iris
tangles of browned blades?

No—I can chart my island
under sky patterns I rename,
design orchards swelling with novel fruit.

At home, the susurrus of familiar breathing.
Old lovers burrow beneath a downy quilt.
Under the skin, muscles sigh
towards another's chest,
arms entwine
and we listen to song
within our bodies
quieting to inborn
rhythm. Earth eases day through dusk
and the moon approves.

On Fidelity

That young artist,
her pelvis
in crotch-grabbing spandex
sounding tarantaras of flawless
erotic dominance

reads the shriveled apple skins of our faces
as a text titled "them"
jack-and-jill-gone-over-the-hill
born
back then
died
on their marriage bed
and don't even know it.

But we, in her glance revolving
at us and past us, recall

round-cheeked you-and-me
scrubbed, dutiful, seated
thigh-beside-thigh concealing
pity for elders

while a tangle of neurons ignited a fuse
speeding towards

exquisite
inexhaustible
beginning.

Afternoon Rite

water scalding
gold to amber

sharp fragrant clove
intimate words

shall I pour you?
out of white glazed

porcelain, sound
of waterfall

whirlpooling spoon
lips at the rim

warmth of a breath
cools the steaming

Sleeping in Half a Bed

i

The one at home had sunk a central niche
after decades, and besides, we had room
for luxury of queen-size level-pitched
space to drift creating separate dreams.

A dozen brass-railed beds, tufted mattress
shown on each, sanitarily zipped plastic.
To bed ourselves in public embarrassed.
The smart saleswoman left us breathing-space.

Horizontal side by side, shoes pointed
to the ceiling, we tried them all in turn.
Too hard—too soft—until at last jointly
knew—just right, bought it even when we learned

the high price. We slept enfolded, or side
by side, our comfort true, until you died.

ii

My dreams have lost their logic since you died.
Logic? Dream-play equals weird, surreal.
The fun of finding truth in what's implied
by images of travel, labyrinthine turmoil,

singing birds, faces recognized or strange.
At times, you're in the cast, part of the scene,
alive and taken for granted, exchanging
past talk in tandem with the might-have-been.

Astonished to awake. Well, we all go
through this deliberate work of the mind.
Bless our brains' electrical modes,
neurons able to envision when blind.

Mind, like a field enriched by lying fallow,
scatters seeds of lyric to fill the hollows.

Crossing the Calendar Bridge

    i

The first New Year's Eve without your turning
in grateful wonder: "Lucky us, we've earned
another year." The mirror on the wall
granted pardon: throughout life's judgment-hall,

one question persisted: "Why am I here?"
Name: doctor, mentor, science pioneer,
father—and sorcerer who alchemized
state-of-loneliness into you-and-I.

We laughed at a third in bed—our snug down
quilt—*perinyeh*—in childhood mother-tongue.
Light as a ghost but warm, the featherbed
rises and falls with my uncertain breaths.

If I could say "he's in a better place"
might I foretell his welcoming embrace?

ii

I did not always welcome his embrace.
Corralled in a split-level—breathing space
defined by husband/children schedules,
reassured by unwritten "good-girl" rules.

No studio—my clattery machine labored
under window with view of the neighbor's
house wall. Marriage, like a boat poised at anchor
unswayed by flickering ripples of rancor,

kept us safe. Yet rhythm known in my bones
formed instrument, mute raised, like saxophone
riffs that tumbled into words. And we sang
off-key, happy, lyrics in differing language.

Our rhymes were true or near or simply free.
Five stages of grief compose an elegy.

iii

Five stages of grief line up for elegy:
deny   rant   reproach   barter   and agree
to let you go, to cease reenacting
hot/cold days/nights of vigil. To distract

mind from memory's sweated matted strings,
loosen knots, twirl his-and-her wedding rings
doubled on one finger, kiss them for luck,
and recognize the shape of me, unbroken.

Not to muse "if only you were here"
as the glittering ball slides down Times Square.
Get past the calendar, switch off the screen
stop conjugating "is" as "might have been."

Yet how to tell the poem "don't reminisce"
all moments lived are sparks to genesis.

Dream Spies

Dreams send intimate informants
my personal crew of spies
who tease me with bits
and pieces

of mirror. As I lie dormant
REM sleep quivering closed eyes
theater opens   hits
and misses

slapstick comedies that torment
suitcase falls open   goldfish
drowns in air   mother knits
burial dress

I've crashed a smoking room for men
only. Am I in disguise?
I'm offered benefits
a free pass

Dreams hire an all-night doorman
for an electric door   sky-high
sliding in place. It's
an address

I can't quite read   windblown form in
sand   strange gods revise
clues to infinites
tides erase.

Where I Live Now

Tall Janet's cane sounds a jangle of keys
Melvin keeps time to a thud as he seizes
the wooden handle of his, rubber-tipped, sorely
needed on carpet or linoleum floor.

A third leg evolves for many here.
Zigzagged by Peter, motorized, who steers
with childhood memory of rides, back-to-back
cars going bump/whizz/crash on crazy tracks.

"You walk so fast!" Who, me? Speed, as they say,
is relative. Each life soap opera played
commercial-free. No reaching eighty-plus
without a house a child a husband lost.

Voices alter, rasp, quaver in the throat.
Talk drives the oars of our humming lifeboat.

Dried Reeds

Beside the stillwater pond
stands of tall reeds lift
feathery end-of-season plumes.
I pull one out—

From the stalk's unbendable spine,
long blades curve outward,
serrated edges
threatening skin.
Best take care, I heal slowly now.
Tears evaporate quickly
and eyes grow hot.

The seed head shakes like a cheerleader's
rattle, bristles like tiny insects with mouths
seeking food powdery as pollen
blown on capricious winds.
Perhaps it is pollen
they open for—the task assigned to them—
make more of yourselves.

Each thread curls, clings
round my finger—does not let go.
Am I parent, child, potential victim?
Is this plant a dissolver
of living animal cells—
its paleness speaks
ghosts morbidity death.

Five and a half months since my beloved
lost color, softness. I wore a yellow
gauze germ-protective smock,
rubber gloves to caress him
at his final sighing vowel
neither oh   nor   ah.

Odor of life insists within
this feathery plume—proof
of wet earth where worms
prowl in comfort.
Fallen pine needles
decay to brown sponge,
solace underfoot
where he and I walk
in infinite bio-botanic
conversion.

II

Secret Model

> In 1986 the art world was stunned by disclosure of a major body of works by the renowned American artist Andrew Wyeth—240 drawings, watercolors, and tempera paintings made over a fifteen year period—all of which had the same subject: Helga Testorf, a neighbor in Chadd's Ford, Pennsylvania.

Comes a day in February when sun
sends a broom to the packed snow and you know
melting's begun. To the sudden sharp
crack of a twig, warmth brushes your cheek.
It's the kind of day that draws you out
into the walking. Two things I do—I walk
and I weave. Not many weave what they wear
any more. But I like to wrap myself
in work of my hands, to finger a nub
and know that was the place the yarn turned
on itself and I coupled two frayed ends.

"The loom's your instrument," he said, "like strings
of a harp. You're part of my instrument
with pencil and brush."

                           Pencil, quick and slow,
crosshatched the ones of me at the loom.
Patience you'd seen only in the hooded
back of an owl or a tensely crouched cat
about to leap, claw, jaw, tear and swallow.
Dangerous almost, as though he breathed me
into charcoal or oil. He kept a good fire
in the studio and an electric heater,
but I never needed more heat than his
fever, working inches away.

                            No talk—
sounds creating a spell   rustle tap rasp.
Patient as God. Each one of the thousand
hairs of my braid giving off light.

Now the world has that moment of us
where he placed me lying naked in spring
foliage—the fallen brown-leafed branch
covers me like an arm, white-pink body
shows like sap flow inside a young tree,
the secret motion fingertips can't reach.
Complete mound of my sex, that tender red
he used for vaginal lip.
                        How could I be
just a woman after he'd transformed me
into cycles of the earth? Rain was in me, sun
and birth.
            I swear it was his pulse alone
that made me come as he went on painting
layers over canvas. I felt flayed, like the Visible
Woman in the science hall—red arteries
blue veins purple nerves organs pumping—
a portrait forcing me into unwilling
truths. I couldn't escape any more
than landscape—solid wood of an oak
was vulnerable as skin to the burn
of his eyes and fingers.
                        I keep the one
no one has seen—nude erect between
white birch saplings, on a summer walk.
I touch the dry-brushed canvas, fine scars
where flesh healed open wound into secret.

Three El Greco Portraits
Metropolitan Museum of Art

Life-size, their eyes
fix to our progress
within hushed walls.

Near-naked
the crucified
not quite of earth white
flesh ascendant
descending
into an empty grave
Touch me if you doubt.

The Cardinal
glows in luxurious red
hands white as a dead man's
enthroned within rites
of bonebreaking
iron nails.
black-rimmed gaze
Bend low to prove your worth.

The artist
long-bodied half-twisted
follows each moving form
step by step
in judgment
of locus
in the composition
Come, you belong to me.

Ukiyo-e, Beauty in Woodblock Print

Blossoming pod of hair inclines
baring her nape, butterfly comb
alights, kimono a foaming
lift of wave, ankle suggested.
The curve of her form beckons—
gestural line the Western eye
reads as letter S.
                                 The artist,
tracing text inscribed on air, reads
her outline as a character
invented for his alphabet
of pleasure—hyphen-eye, pin-mouth,
L of nose, earlobe an accent
drifted from a waning moon.

The man who buys the print will fix
his gaze upon luminous crushed
jewel stones rendering open
peonies. Her powdered skin
stirs thoughts of climbing a lattice,
fingers tapping the drawn panel
of an embroidered silken screen.
He visits her at will, his flesh
aroused by collector's delight.

Rauschenberg's Goat
A "combine" by Robert Rauschenberg

There are no sadder colors than red and yellow
daubs on a blue face
found down in the dumps
the hit-and-run damaged snout
clown-patched

blotches of gouache
applied by a makeup artist
the goat in death readied
for carnival

Longhaired silvery wool
brushed to shine
like a thoroughbred stud's
burnishing its owner's vanity

Horns spiral outward in ideal symmetry.
It must have backed into the tread-worn
rubber tire belly-bracelet
and landed with hooves
glued upon tattered
throwaway texts
newspapers   posters   admission tickets

Coffined
within a glass cube

The Show Goes On

The Mollusc World
Aquarium, Monterey, California

At noon, the great Hand
breaches World's undulating membrane
and a jet of pellets
arouses a swarm of yellow bee fish.
Coarser pellets meander
awaited by the o-mouthed
blackeyed rockfish who waves transparent ruffled fins
like a drag queen in summer georgette
having wiggled its lump of backside into a hole in the reef
drilled by acid suction of a geoduck clam's
feeding tube, a plasmatic human-sized phallus.
The clam, spent,
revolving with tidal currents
will stumble across virgin coral.

On the sandy bottom
striped angel wings
refill muscular bellies
raking nutrients through toothed gums.
All dross drifts to spiral-humped moon snails
who cleanse by grazing—
devourer-plows
patient in dim light

where shadows of spectators
swim the glass shield
in a dream of regaining
so gentle a fit.

Hall of Mammalian Life
American Museum of Natural History, New York City

Fifty years—the gorilla family tableau
alive as in my childhood
    baby at mother's breast,
    nearby an aunt,
    cabbage-green leaf
    hanging from her lower lip.
    The male fist-pounding his chest.
I'd sneak a look on my way out
but never caught them out of pose.

82nd Street
Dancer-slim mother,
    her chattering sprite, tawny mane swinging,
    flanked by two Golden Labradors.
Jaywalker teen, long nails flower-painted
    digging into a styrofoam cup
    mining chicken nuggets.

Starbuck's passion fruit iced tea
    buys me the right to a green table.
Woman with toddler climbing her backpack
    angles a plaid stroller
    through revolving door blades.

Was I that young woman?
Cities I've lived in
burn through decades of scorched calendars.

The gorillas cage time
in their forest glade.
Collectors kill with care
not to tear the bristled skin.

Hatshepsut, Woman Pharoah
Metropolitan Museum of Art

Three thousand years of wind-packed sands
ripple to the wakening
of a sun-god
trashed into fragments.
Lion-warm grains
buffer crevices.
Rose-granite shards
like cells fitted each to each
breathe in the dark.

Patient fingers
stroke with quills
soft brushes   fine sieves
reconnect layers of girl-body
seated with royal bull's tail
between thighs

restore a woman-face   serene
round cheeks   pointed chin
        wearing the Pharaoh's
        signifying beard
full lips
at peace with a sculptor-slave.

Visitors approach like supplicants
in the museum throne room

Static-scratch of audioguides
Hum of captions read aloud

to oddly silent children
damp fingers twisting
parents' jacket hems

blinking into eyes
that have never known lids.

Writers' Museum
Edinburgh, Scotland

Yellowed goose-quill, splay at the point,
Sepia scriptings, needle-thin, faint,
Pages foxed. Any common thing—
Eye glass, cravat, tobacco purse, ring.
Imbued with writer's sweat or breath
Sealed in a glass box, life in death.
Barbered curls on coffin velvet,
Auburn snips—Burns, Sir Walter Scott.

Here the corruptible essence
Glows without light, phosphorescence
Bred of self. Relics glisten, speak.
Organs excised, a black-eyed hawk
Nailed to a cherrywood book shelf
Claws a hapless ripple of pelt.
Speckled feathers animate fill,
Belly-stuff of attic rag doll.

Poets' ink as well as blood pulsates.
A pebble scratches chalk on slate.
Eyes in portraits memorize, watch,
Take note. Stitch by sensory stitch
The quill pricks like a tailor's hook
Seamless rhyme in a music book.
The painted mill framed on the wall
Glitters with droplets in free fall

Roar of the river, wheel of stone.
Gather the grain their seeds have sown.

Sculptor

Her hands move in accord
with idle desire
led by mind, a palimpsest,
retracing patterns.

A hand-sawed stump,
brown as a beaver's tail,
glints as though wary eyes
open in secret.

The root seems to expose
a petrified half-buried snake.
In the smoothness of annual rings,
she decodes a wheel of first motion,
seed's taste of air, water,
dusks clamoring into dawns.

In hot sun at noon, splinters burn.
Bark peels, shreds fall away.
The heartwood smells of ferment.
Dying's no passive matter.
Regeneration takes work.

III

Sight Loss

This is the final day of years of sweetness
of color-quick ways of knowing.

Whose are the faces I no longer
understand at a glance? Voice

offers child/woman/man but
if stranger/friend chooses silence?

My reaching hands slice nothingness
body careens through an opened door

lands scrabbling on a stoop
hearing derision.

Am I bleeding? This is
our kitchen where the ceiling

recognizes percussive footsteps
of upstairs neighbors.

Warm stir in the air   I lay
ear to your heartbeat.

Let my tongue bless
the tips of your fingers

try gentle bristles of your chin
to your mouth. Oh,

from this day you must
flavor your pity with honey

that I may see yesterday's light
with my lips.

The Amsler Grid Test

A square enclosing squares
as on graph paper,
in its center, a critical black dot

meant to mirror the pupil of your eye.
Just a boring game until one day
the lines mimic tangled wire

and the horizontal slats of window blinds
crimp in the middle like a sheaf of wheat.
The roof across the street

dances the shadow of a fringe
over your forehead,
and you envy the canine sense by which

some breeds appraise the world
through a fall of feathery fur,
an obstacle

made up for by sniffing
mightily at strangers,
licking fingers that have sorted food.

Bless all stoic seeing-eye dogs
and those whose hands
seek their halters.

Seven-Day Candle

Choosing sin over chance of fire
I blow out the flame burning in a glass cylinder
on my fifth day of mourning.

Hardening wax coats
the blue sixpointed star
above the letters In Memoriam.

Blackened wick quivers in a pool of melt.
Have I hobbled my father's soul?

Sweater

For his 90th birthday, I bought
a sweater-vest the color of Lake Como's
blue interplay of snow-covered peaks
ceremonious clouds and fjord-deep water

with carved leather buttons
and wishbone cables
straight as the braids I used to wind
round my head in a crown.

Not another minute could I stand
his threadbare cardigan—
the one my mother knitted
thirty years back
> *I don't knit to save money,*
> *cheap yarn isn't worth my work*

But now a mustardy map of stains,
odd matchups to lost buttons
he'd sewn with thread from a prewar
spool of thick black cotton,

his "old faithful" worn indoors
and out, thrown over
pajamas during hospital emergencies.
He clutched it round his body

like a man housed in a cardboard box,
though he had lived to become
sought after by women in the Home
desiring his gallant arm.

I remember my mother's
color-coded aluminum needles,
the sibilance of tap-and-brush
as her unswerving fingers
tilted at that four-ply wool.
Awkward at English scripted letters,
her stitches rhymed without fault.
Summa cum laude of yarnover loops,

commas and tildes of knit and purl,
she cast off chains of parentheses.
A zippered bolero jacket for me at twelve,
wool like curly brown persian lamb
It'll be warm for you like a peltzele, a fur.

"Time, Dad,
to wear the new sweater, don't you think?"
"Why, this one's still very comfortable—
plenty of good service left."

When, at 100, he dies,
I clear out his dresser.
Tissue paper crisp as dry ice
opens to pristine blue.

The vest fits my torso and frees my arms
every winter day
inside my chilly house. The pockets

accommodate kleenex, keys,
my watch and rings when hands
plunge into meat or dough,
trying to coax raw mixtures into forms.

Like any good part of my body,
the sweater allows me
to forget its existence
while I work at my desk

adding blue linked loops
to my life with a pen.

Tell Me the Names You Don't Know

What does one inherit when an estranged brother dies? Cold
hands, heart thump, ruffle of snapshots. Unknown
children, grandchildren. From Tennessee, the voice of a nephew
>My daughter Rachel wants to construct a family tree.
>Do you know the name of the town
>your mother came from?

A tree? Careful—to graph my family history, crosshatch
a broken staircase—risers of ancient gravestones,
illegible Semitic consonants.

Kaminetz Bidolsk   leaps from my lips.
>How is it spelled?
Transliterated from Yiddish, from Polish, who knows?
>Could I find it on the map?
It was a shtetl, and no longer exists.

>What was her father's name, mother, siblings?
Mordka, Freda, brother Nuchim had children.
>Their names?
All killed save one—my dear first cousin
Rochel who turned up in Israel.

>My daughter's asking did they burn the houses?
My cousin Rochel doesn't talk about it, and I don't ask.
>I'll try the internet.
Do you know that your daughter carries my mother's name?
>No, your mother's name was Rose!
In America. Her birth name was Rochel, which is Rachel.

He doesn't call again, but I climb
fractured rungs of a stairway
where Jacob dreams with open eyes of a name
we know as Rachel or Rahel.
Spell ch or h for the throaty aspirate
English chokes on. History
written in letters of light leads to a well
and the goatskin
Rachel lowered and drew up full.

Tell Me, Brother Dying

Olympic racer surgeons strap you down,
intubate, inject, surround the table
while out of body overhead you've flown
with eyes open. Resurrection fable

leads you through a megaphone of light
humming with songs keyed to distant voices.
And now you pass warm welcomers—burial site
letters of stone revived by childhood's faces.

Tell me—who's there? Your long gone fawning
Stan, clown of the playground? He burst apart
at Saigon, drafted for war in the dawn's
early light. They assigned you a desk—your heart's

congenital murmur saved you. Teachers?
Miss Ennis? At home you set me giggling
when you mimicked her skinny arm itching
to mark F's on your left-handed squiggle.

Who shades a brow, squinting? Does Mother,
puzzled, complain about the glaring beam?
Will you sing "Row Your Boat" with Father?
His baritone led "Life is but a dream."

"Give me a topic sentence," I would ask,
"what can I write about The Magic Mountain?"
"This book is about fevered people who bask
in cold sun, breathing with lungs like dry fountains."

A button's pressed—the ventilator trails
your final sigh. Tell me, brother dying,
will you someday lead, young hand on my failing
aged wrist, lift me, without wings, flying?

Moving to a Smaller Home, I Give Up My H.D./Bryher Collection

Motion-sickness—looking
up / down my library wall
listing those by or about
two divers into the whirlpool
we call high modernism.

Each book I must now give away
presses between the covers
a scrap of time lived in pages

like a pebble tossed into a crevice
discovered to be a bud
pushing open

flaring into sunlight.
There, look, two women,
their powers a balm,
pages alive with telling
how they wrote   endured   loved

Shared vision
grown so clear I could see
my pencilled notes

as though traced
over carbon impressions
and hear
once in a while

my silences
discover
tone, pitch, and key.

Stillness at 3:00 A.M.

I wake to a moment
of light
like a held breath

and continuance.
That gesture,
derived from earth's rotation,
speaks to me as promise

beyond glass mosaic
figures outlined in black
who deliver us
to self-reproach
by their storied suffering.

I choose
not to be burdened
as the abused child
loves and loves and craves
love the only way it knows.

Moonlight scrolls over surf
   writing   erasing
word that might have been
the beginning

Flood Washed

On the asphalt lies a question mark
two feet long—

brown mosaic triangles, beige stripes,
narrow head.

With reluctant thumb and forefinger
I spin it

over, belly down. A fatal slit
down the side.

Bird's beak, perhaps. If alive, just
its sliding

stir would have chilled to shiver.
Pity now,

and curiosity. Pretty—
so pretty—

how could Eve—or I—not be lured?
Glossy coat,

graceful neck. "Snake!" our children
in terror,

had raced from the backyard bushes.
Young husband-

father dug his hoe, down and down.
Conqueror,

protector of household and clan
from beauty.

Who framed you, the visionary
poet asks—

from whence comes this earthly design
built into

matter's insistent desire: In
all things, form.

IV

News of the Day Pantoum

How many to count until final peace?
Morning papers print tallies by nation
Keyboards chatter of hostage release
Familiar words re-appear in translation

Morning papers print tallies by nation
A dozen today blown up on patrol
"Purity" "Cleansing" re-appear in translation
Rice Krispies swell in my breakfast bowl

Two dozen today blown up on patrol
The Times arrives in a plastic bag
Rice Krispies swell in my breakfast bowl
Newsprint smudges the shell of my egg

The Times arrives in a plastic bag
Does water mean life existed on Mars?
Newsprint smudges the shell of my egg
Oil drills on tundra follow north stars

Does water mean life existed on Mars?
Bewildering sunspots flare strobes in the sky
Oil drills on tundra follow north stars
Diving bells flash-photo undersea night

Bewildering sunspots flare strobes in the sky
Every night I recycle newspaper
Diving bells flash-photo undersea night
Black holes swallow stars burnt to vapor

Every night I recycle all paper
Keyboards chatter of prisoner release
Black holes swallow stars burnt to vapor
One, and then one, until the final peace.

Split Screen

to bless say *kaddish*
        for severed finger shred
of navel phlegm of brain
        purple that may be spleen
a child's toenail gleams
        fish scale in the searchlight

                women's faces a row of oval windows
                    framed in black headshawls
            boys fisting shards of concrete
                dodging broken pipes   water
          in arterial gush   bodies atwist
              on shattered glass

eye in the palm of a rubber glove
        king among the blind
tongue torn from psalm of praise
        b'eit hashem how to
pick out the heart of the suicide
        aquiver with heaven

            tank cannons
                    eyeless in gaza
        muezzin's *allaah* rises through dust
                marketplace a street
    to kiss   and kiss
              in mourning

If I forget thee
        oh Jerusalem
        oh Bethlehem

Awakening, She

speeds to the click-world's magnetic confetti spinning her into a void
of connection glance-bys from never-mets cryptic codes flaming
insults do you too have celiac chronic fatigue syndrome hiv pixel
glints of seas engulfing icebergs calving empty bee hives tarred oil
body counts

among

cool meadows of openly given intellect wildflower scattering of trust
try this lead click/text extrasolar stars names for the lights we sail
past auroral colors exploding particles of the spectrum exquisite
smoke of burntout suns

links to her hollow of homelessness rib-locked opaque in bone
embrace circled by flashing digits quick fingers propel while eyes
forget to blink

Tell Me, Pretty Maiden, Are There Any More at Home Like You?

Geno-Infinity National Bank opens at the posted hour. Voices in C major may I may I help I help the next next person person person person? Thrum of thank you you you have a nice day day day stereophonic underbeat to electronic churr telephonic purr rubbershoe shuffle.

Revolving floor propels towards U of grilled windows sounds of keyboard tap and brush fingernails enamelled variant lacquered symbols
dollar, pound, mark, shekel, yen, lire, franc, peso, drachma, groschen, ruble, guilder, euro, rand..

Duplicate lipsticked smiles, whitened incisors, love of self ingrained in muscle, brain and nerve cells, nucleus one cell of ritahayworth technicolor auburn cascading dance-drilled shoulders
may I may I help I help the next next person person person person

In sweet sorority on weekends they switch-fool men pre-ordered, novelty of sexual tastes chiming shrill night tones exchanged in the cubicled sleeping loft may I may I help you thank you yes oh next next may I thank you oh yesyesohyes

Keyboards sputter plastic tag admission to interactive catalog, touch-scroll sex, height, weight, color, entitlement per value accrued in your account. Engender free choice in line with root network, any such as bicolor split/albino fur/finned tail. Insert card, remove in twenty seconds green-arrow chip as you wish as you wish as you wish as you wish as you wish

Proceed to interlacing neon tubes, surrender chip to first available identical male technician, await projected infant, child or adult, one to three hours according clicked complexities of trait
as you wish as you wish as you as you as you

Sea Chantey

As a child I knelt
with cupped hands
to catch flickers of fish
transparent as the water
sounding   shush   shush
like memories of ancient prayer.

The morning surf spills ocherous foam.
Oil on a wave's twitching back
tars the feathers
of famished gulls
struggling to mount the wind.

Children run on our sands of denial
and slake thirsts
with numbing bubbles
bottled in plastic
the colors of jellyfish

cast like reliquary offerings
dutiful currents
ferry back to shore.

Milton's Daughters

To monitor Eden with eyes gone blind
he consecrated his duty-bound daughters
to heaven/hell marriage. Two shiver-spined
spinsters iced in the swirling lamp-black water

of Father's inkwell, transformed into quills
scratching rhythms of his larynx hoarse
with prophesying shout. They brought hot meals,
then poured chamber slops out at night. Remorse

never misted fires of a brilliant brain
of metrical philosophies composed
for girl-fingers worn to nubs, whorls of stain
they scrubbed with homemade lye while Father dozed.

Filial devotions their only defenses,
remembered by epithet—amanuensis.

Inside/Outside: Gurgaon, India

Inside the glass-walled tower
morning yawns on flowered quilts.
Faucets rush clear falls
over glowing bodies.
                The glass is soundproof
                to the voice of a boy
                who upends
                a bucket of gutter water
                over his head
                down washboard ribs.
Forest bird songs
trill from spinning discs.
                Heat thickens
                staccato
                cries shrill and hoarse
                sirens   barking dogs
                choked off.
Paths of beige and orange tile
traverse the atrium
to the white-columned school's
keyboards and modems.
Elevators rise
and descend.
                Beings with bowed bones
                and scabbed skin
                try to climb the sheer vertical,
                lay hollow bellies to the glass,
                dessicate parts
                cling like worn moths.
Sunset mauves darkening
silk carpets
signal the night's

click-on of lights.
                        A guard with powerful hose
                        sluices the glass wall's detritus
                        into the street.

Beggars, We Pray in Flood

There is no high ground though I cling to the trees
Waters rise in fury and filth, calm them, lord, please

Wasim and Shelaba torn from my arms
Keep my innocents' heads above water, lord, please

My mother and father too old to swim
Float them to shore and in solace, lord, please

A handful of sticks is the house where we slept
in one bed—a roof and a floor, lord, please

Presidents and ministers drone overhead
magnify babies' cries to their ears, lord, please

We lived in nirvana and did not know -
Maryam, Atif, Jawad, Sima, Rahil, lord, please.

Abel, the First Funeral

Entwine large-leafed vine,
sheath him well. In death,
wrap with life. Stem-sap
laves, scents. Fresh green saves,
eases eyes, teases
memories, stories.
Braid a cord to each side.
Scale horizontal
ground to his length. Pound
clay, sever roots. Lay
what was, and is not,
softly down. The rough
walls powder and fall.

Brothers are authors:
civil war's alive.

v

New Child

born of woman and anonymous donor

Aura from uncharted space spiraled
to where a warm pulse
beat within salt-sweet waters

Fingers unweb
to touch in time the lips
of two loving women
and a sister child

You tell us of ethereal life
resonant with music
as a pedal holds all notes of a chord
on and on until a string vibrates
O
new scale of possibility

In your kicking sucking pushing self
retain that memory
of infinite unceasing
motion

May you help us compose a psalm
garnered from galaxies unseen
by human telescope

No one brought you but the stars
beyond our day's
sphere of night

Revelation
in memoriam J.S.

You dived for us into night-dark
bringing mysteries to light—
harlequin and psychedelic
kaleidoscopic explosions
gliding through branches of living coral—
the eight-armed   the finned
creatures who breathe salt waters in the way
that we who clomp noisily
on rock sand and pavement
depend on wind-carried air.

In mask and goggles
wearing a backpack of oxygen
you hunted the strange and beautiful
not with knife, net, or gun
but with a camera
brought them up to our earth
to live
as incandescent prints and slides
magically projected.

And on our landed world
you hunted wild blossomings
to transplant and nurture
beside your front door.

I do not dive into saltwater depths,
gaze only at surfaces—
sunlit ripples breaking into jewels,
horizon on gray days
blending sky with sea.
I pick up shells, find quivering jellyfish
surf discards onto sand,
follow sights and sounds
of shore birds, blur of sandpiper legs,
harsh calls of gulls

and thanks to you,
know ocean and garden
veiled from daily view.

Martha's Vineyard

Cars like a litter of mongrels
nuzzle the seagrass rim of the cove.

Trailing our hosts
we set up a row of shortlegged
canvas chairs and face the water
each with a book angled
on jack-knifed knees.

Quiet rules this blue saucer.
No wind-eroded cliffs
or crashing breakers.
Sibilant surf,
tidal broomstraws stirring
unbroken shells.

Seven white gulls
bob like inflated bath toys
A windsurfer labors his single wing
striped in purple and flamingo pink.

On the sand a lone gull
prints a cuneiform track
towards me on reedy legs
crop bulging.
Fingerlings dart staccato feast
in the bay. Feeding's easy
for both of us this weekend

guests of the vineyard.
I tip my straw hat, admire
the way the filled pouch of his body
idles in the sun

wingless, so smoothly
do resting feathers conform.

Beachcomber

Blue stone, violet spiral shell,
Souvenirs of summer in my hand,
Salt relics of our last farewell.
Blue stone, violet spiral shell,
Sea-tumbled fragments cast a spell,
Brown glass a tiger's eye in sand.
Blue stone, violet spiral shell,
Souvenirs of summer in my hand.

The Pond

Follow the dance—a fountain sprays
upward, white waterfall that plays
concentric ripples. Surface sheen
reflects the grass and evergreens.
Shadowy fish pass under glaze.

I come to sit on this bench and gaze
across to the woods on clear days
as high-necked geese paddle and preen,
follow the dance.

A fish leaps up, gold in sun's rays—
unwary dragonfly has grazed
too close to the alluring screen.
Stands of cattails dip to the scene.
My notebook enters words of praise,
follows the dance.

Oak Tree Chronicle

Oak leaves hang on, blithely outride
the wind, swaying dun-colored, dried.
Acorns scatter in jazzy rounds
of random drumming on the ground,
the squirrels' come-and-get-it guide.

Though almost in tatters beside
birches gorgeous in gold as brides
papery yellows swirling down,
oak leaves hang on.

School kids shuffle kicking sky high
red mauve confetti as they glide
laugh and leap into crackling sounds.
Hickory, maple, jumbled mounds
raked and vacuumed, dumped, nullified.
Oak leaves hang on.

November, Woman and Birds

Close as rain
they form black-
speckled clouds of din.

Out of summer heat
on the lee side of rock
between tideline and dune

wings in first flight
scour the air in unison.
How do they read the paths in sky?

Street corner gusts of wind
spin signs into an argument
        One Way—>
        <—One Way

Friends are loading their vans
heading south single file
honking horns in goodbye.

The woman zipped into red fleece
checks direction by the quill
of nerve that pricks her cheek

as the wind sails her
to her windowed brick cube
sealed against the seasons.

At the Vernal Equinox

Spring? My studio's a chilly catacomb
bricked with spines of poetry for walls.
Raise the thermostat to a higher number?
Hot flashes of guilt burn with fossil fuels.

We're told Earth's wearing out—twisters, floods, drought—
that lakes and rivers generate gilled brutes
devouring fish we'll learn to do without,
that squawkers render songbirds nestless, mute.

Stubborn, my body's chilled hormonal gauge
signals vessels stiff with arterial rust,
rattled nerves skate on window glass besieged
by berserk fifty mile an hour gusts.

But today's the equinox—yang marries yin.
Night equals day—grab a sweater and grin.

Autumn Walk in a Gated Garden
for Vincent

Open the gate of weathered wood to invisible
strollers observing sun moon stars.
Leafless twigs bare nodes of blossom.
Breathe the sounding spray of waterfall.

Walk the papery crush of pine needles.
A single hibiscus trembles, old flower
unsought by summer bees, white-winged frill flaccid,
yet inner purple flares, yellow stamen defiant.

Descend past spiked clusters of laurel,
follow the clamor frothing over rocks
cascading to a wide round pond's concentric circles
dotted by gold buds of fish and watchful frogs.

Stone formation guards the pool like a lion couchant, easeful power
where water rock and trees intertwine
place in the universe.
A stone slab bridges the stream.

A stand of slender oak shades the second gate,
circle inside a square frame.
A small ancient boat awaits.
Sail into ultimate center where water springs upwards and renews.

The third gate of solid seasoned wood conceals what lies beyond.
Rusted iron latch and pull rings will not open today.
Let the garden teach patience
in changes of earth, water, rock, wind,

the play of wills between starved ground,
a straggle of skeletal trees,
and a gardener who said,
"Let there be this."

Spilled White

Some kinds of beauty require
no labor. The kindness of a snowfall
purifies my yard

until untimely melt
re-stages front and center
what I'd forgot of
drought-killed lawn with, worse,
storm-hacked branch debris.

Nature as cyclical pruner
understands triage—cut
splintery junctures,
save nutrient for roots.

Our bodies don't have such talent
although Amazon women, they say,
would slice the pillowy swell of a breast
in trade for freed arm muscle.

My mother is departed
and is the world shapelier?

Departures list on timetables.
Does the scheme of my life
stamp a date on my passport?

What invisible monitor assigns
aisle, middle, window?

Shall I board the silent plane or
ski the clouds below
solid as snow.

Charlotte Mandel is winner of the 2012 New Jersey Poets Prize awarded by *Journal of New Jersey Poets*. She has published seven previous books of poetry, the most recent *Rock Vein Sky* from Midmarch Arts Press. Other titles include two poem-novellas of feminist biblical re-vision—*The Life of Mary*, with foreword by Sandra M. Gilbert, and *The Marriages of Jacob*. Other awards include two fellowships in poetry from New Jersey State Council on the Arts; Woman of Achievement Award (Arts) from NJ Business and Professional Women; The Writer's Voice, NYC; residencies at Yaddo, including a Geraldine R. Dodge fellowship; Millay Colony; Virginia Center for the Creative Arts; Montalvo Arts Center. Her verse play "The Gardener's Wife" appears in the print and online journal *Verse Wisconsin*. She founded and coordinated the Eileen W. Barnes Award for older women poets and edited the anthology, *Saturday's Women*. As an independent scholar, she has published a series of articles on the role of cinema in the life and work of poet H.D. She recently retired from teaching poetry writing at Barnard College Center for Research on Women. Visit her at www.charlottemandel.com.